INVESTIGATE!
UNDERSTANDING GOD

Original French text © 2018 Sophie de Mullenheim
Illustrations © 2018 Sophie Chaussade
English translation by Deborah Lock
This edition copyright © 2021 Lion Hudson IP Limited

Published by
Lion Hudson Limited
Wilkinson House, Jordan Hill Business Park
Banbury Road, Oxford OX2 8DR, England
www.lionhudson.com

ISBN 978 0 74597 945 8

Original edition published in French under the title Enquête sur Dieu by Sophie de Mullenheim (text) and Sophie Chaussade (Illustrations)
Enquête sur Dieu © First published in French by Mame, Paris, France - 2018
First English language edition 2021

Acknowledgments
Bible quotations taken from the Holy Bible, New International Version Anglicised. Copyright © 1979, 1984, Biblica, formerly International Bible Society. Used by permission of Hodder & Stoughton Ltd, an Hachette UK company. All rights reserved. "NIV" is a registered trademark of Biblica. UK trademark number 1448790.

The Publisher would like to thank Claire Clinton
Director of Religious Education and RSHE, RE Matters Ltd.

A catalogue record for this book is available from the British Library
Printed and bound in China, February 2021, LH54

Sophie de Mullenheim • Sophie Chaussade

INVESTIGATE!
UNDERSTANDING
GOD

THE CHRISTIAN FAITH

LION
CHILDREN'S

and THOMAS SOPHIE
MYSTERIOUS...
GREAT! AN INVITATION!
For Thomas
POST BOX
THOMAS, I AM INVITING YOU TO MY FIRST COMMUNION. 25 MAY AT CHURCH 11 A.M. SOPHIE
DAD, SOPHIE HAS INVITED ME TO HER FIRST COMMUNION. WHAT IS IT? IS IT A BIRTHDAY?
NO, I THINK SOPHIE WILL EAT THE BODY OF CHRIST.
SOPHIE, A CANNIBAL? MYSTERIOUS...
A LITTLE LATER...
GRANDMA, SOPHIE IS HAVING HER FIRST COMMUNION. WHAT IS IT?
JESUS WILL ENTER HER HEART, BUT YOU SHOULD ASK A PRIEST. HE WILL EXPLAIN.
SOPHIE IS HAVING AN OPERATION? STRANGE SHE DIDN'T TELL ME.

CONTENTS

◆ ◆ ◆

1 DOES GOD EXIST?

God, if you exist, answer me!

You... exist...

...answer me!

DO YOU THINK THAT'S AN ANSWER?

Does God exist? If only God answered out loud when this question is asked… If only God appeared from time to time, it would be so much simpler!

VISIBLE GOD

The unique pattern of snowflakes, the spider's web with its perfect design, the human brain capable of the most amazing inventions… Are these not incredible? In fact, many scholars are so amazed at the discoveries they make, they consider only one all-powerful being could have created all of this. Some refer to a "great watchmaker" for just like a watch with many moving parts, nothing so complex as creation could come about by chance. Others speak of a superior intelligence. Christians say it is God. For them, God can be seen everywhere and all the time!

Useful words

Faith: This comes from the Latin *fides*, which means trust. Faith is trust in God. It is faith that helps people to believe.

A WORD OF WISDOM

"Everyone who is seriously involved in the pursuit of science becomes convinced that a spirit is manifest in the laws of the Universe – a spirit vastly superior to that of man, and one in the face of which we with our modest powers must feel humble."

Albert Einstein

Now faith is confidence in what we hope for and assurance about what we do not see. This is what the ancients were commended for.

Hebrews 11:1–2

GOING FURTHER

Why does God not show himself to us more directly? Christians believe in a God that loves all people. God does not force people to love him. This leaves them free to believe in God or not. Anyone who believes in God does so through faith. Christians think that faith is God's gift – a great gift that they never finish unpacking, as discovering more about God, loving, and getting to know God lasts a lifetime.

Yes!

You're here, yes?

✓ TO FIND OUT ABOUT GOD IN THREE PERSONS, GO TO...

7

✓ TO DISCOVER WHAT A RELIGION IS, GO TO...

26

Was the world made IN SEVEN DAYS?

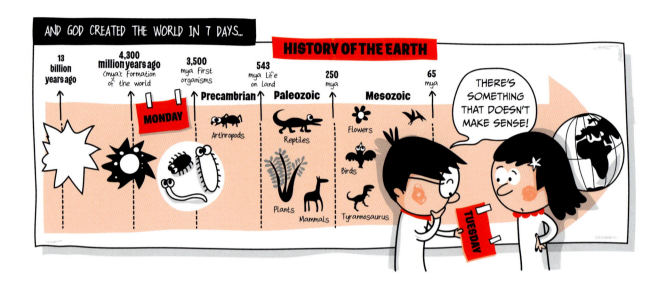

A science book explains that the world was created over billions of years. The Bible, the Christian holy book, begins by telling how God created the world in seven days. Which is right? Some Christians believe that the world was created in seven days by God. Many other Christians believe that both explanations are correct. A science book explains how and the Bible explains why.

WHY, NOT HOW

On the one hand, scientists explain how the process of the world's creation happened. They rely on dates, observations, and calculations. There is still much more to discover… On the other hand, the book of Genesis in the Bible begins with a narrative that explains why the world was made. Christians believe that the world was created by God out of love. Genesis does not provide calculations but measures only the great love of God.

AND WHY…

seven days?
In the Bible, the number 7 symbolizes what is perfect. God created the world over six days, and then on the seventh day God rested and blessed what had been created. God's blessing made the world perfect.

TIMELESS

God does not exist within time, for God created time. Many Christians believe that the account of the seven days of creation in Genesis is not fixed to a timeline as people calculate time. Genesis is not a history or a science book, but a book about beginnings.

MYSTERIOUS...

The beginning of Genesis is not scientific, but it is interesting to notice that the story follows the order of appearance of the species on earth. For example, scientists know that the first animals lived in the water. Then they came out of the water to live on land. In the Bible, God first creates marine animals and then land animals.

WHAT IF WE ADOPTED GOD'S TIME ON SUNDAYS?

✓ TO FIND OUT IF THE BIBLE IS JUST STORIES,
GO TO...
12

✓ TO DISCOVER MORE ABOUT THE CREATION OF PEOPLE,
GO TO...
3

3 DID ADAM AND EVE
really exist?

IN YOUR OPINION, WHO PAINTED THESE DRAWINGS?

ADAM AND EVE!

In the book of Genesis, there is a second creation story about a beautiful garden where the first man and first woman lived with God. Their names were Adam, based on the Hebrew word *adamah* meaning earth, and Eve, from the Hebrew word meaning life. This creation story, like the first one, does not say how and what they looked like, but instead tells about God's plan for humankind.

GOD'S VIPS

The creation narratives show that God is the creator of everything, including humankind. God created humans in his image, which means that people's resemblance to God is not physical, but rather reflects God's love and glory. The story tells how God placed humans in an important position of control, care, and responsibility over all living things.

Useful words

Sin: The Greek word for sin means "to miss the mark", with the mark being God's perfection. It is a wrong thought or action that causes separation from God.

AND WHY...

an apple?

The Bible tells how Adam and Eve disobeyed God by eating the fruit of the tree of knowledge of good and evil that God had told them not to touch. This event is known as the Fall. The first Bibles were written into Latin. The Latin word *malum* means both "evil" and "apple". So, the forbidden fruit became associated with an apple.

MYSTERIOUS...

Scientists talk about species evolving. Humans evolved from a branch close to the chimpanzee, for humans and apes share a common ancestor. Believing in God does not prevent an acceptance of this scientific theory, for the Bible tells about God's relationship with humankind.

LOVED BY GOD

Christians believe that humanity was created to have a special loving relationship with God. In the story of the beginning, God looks at what has been created and finds it good. When God creates humankind, God sees this as very good. Humans are God's masterpiece, most loved by God and free to love God in return. The account shows that humans are not lost in the universe but are the most valuable thing in God's eyes.

AND WHAT DID THE FIRST HUMANS EAT?

APPLES!

✓ TO FIND OUT MORE ABOUT BEING MADE IN THE IMAGE OF GOD, GO TO...

2

✓ TO DISCOVER ABOUT GOD'S FORGIVENESS OF SINS, GO TO...

10

Was Jesus
AN IMAGINARY PERSON?

4

NAME ME SOME IMAGINARY CHARACTERS.

BLUEBEARD

CINDERELLA

AH NO, JESUS IS NOT IMAGINARY. DOES ANYONE KNOW WHY?

JESUS!

BECAUSE HIS STORY DOESN'T START WITH "ONCE UPON A TIME!".

What is the difference between Harry Potter and Anne Frank? The first one was created from the imagination of a writer, and the second one is a person from history. Anne Frank lived and there are accounts of her life. Jesus is also a historical figure. He lived more than 2,000 years ago in an area that is now part of the Middle East. The proof? The accounts of many witnesses.

THE FIRST WITNESSES

Those who lived with Jesus were the first witnesses. They were the twelve chosen disciples, called apostles, and other followers. Two of Jesus' disciples, Matthew and John, wrote about Jesus' life and these are called Gospels in the Bible. The other two

Gospels are written by two men named Luke and Mark. They listened to the accounts of those who knew and met Jesus and wrote down what they

heard. In these four accounts, there are other people such as Herod and Pontius Pilate who are also recorded in history. These accounts provide testimony for the time when Jesus lived. The writers of the Gospels were followers of Christ, so they could be accused of lying…

OR NOT!

There are other witnesses who were not followers of Christ who wrote accounts that included mention of Jesus. These included the Roman politicians Pliny and Tacitus and Jewish historians such as Flavius Josephus. There are so many pieces of historical texts that speak of Jesus that it is hard to say that he did not exist. Historians therefore agree that Jesus existed. But not everyone believes that he was the Son of God, for that requires faith.

AND WHY…

is the calendar based on the year of Jesus' birth?

Originally, the calendar used by the Roman empire was calculated from the time of the foundation of Rome. But in 532, a monk proposed to make the calendar begin at the birth of Jesus. The proposal was adopted, and since then the years on the world's most widely used calendar have been calculated as before or after Jesus Christ. This is often referred to as the Common Era.

A WORD OF WISDOM

"About this time there lived Jesus, a wise man, if indeed one ought to call him a man. For he was one who performed surprising deeds and was a teacher of such people as accept the truth gladly. He won over many Jews and many of the Greeks. He was the Messiah."
Flavius Josephus

DEATH OF TUTANKHAMUN – 1325 BEFORE JESUS CHRIST

DISCOVERY OF HIS TOMB – 1922 AFTER JESUS CHRIST

WITHOUT JESUS THERE WOULD BE FEWER DATES TO REMEMBER!

✓ TO FIND OUT ABOUT THE PEOPLE WHO MET JESUS,
GO TO…
14

✓ TO DISCOVER IF JESUS WAS REALLY BORN ON DECEMBER 25,
GO TO…
15

Map of places

Jesus lived in an area now known as the Middle East on the shores of the Mediterranean Sea. At the time, the land of the Jewish people was occupied by the Romans.

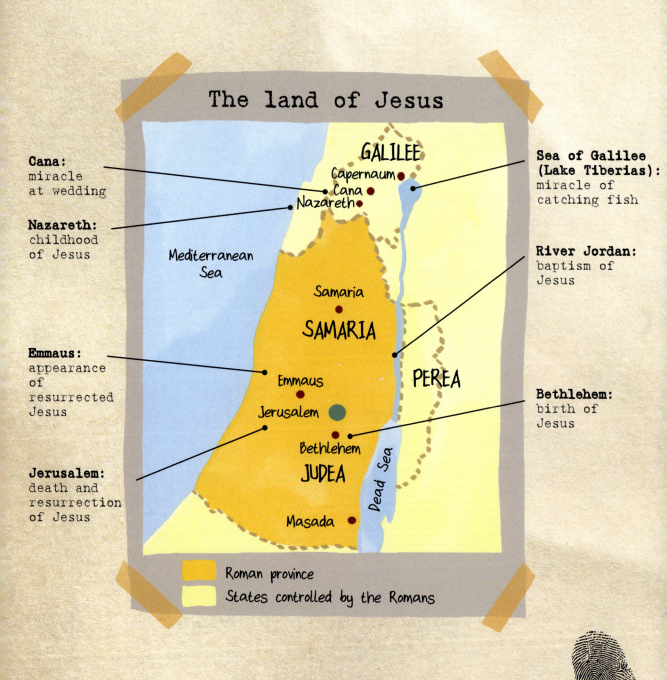

The land of Jesus

Cana: miracle at wedding

Nazareth: childhood of Jesus

Emmaus: appearance of resurrected Jesus

Jerusalem: death and resurrection of Jesus

Sea of Galilee (Lake Tiberias): miracle of catching fish

River Jordan: baptism of Jesus

Bethlehem: birth of Jesus

GALILEE

Capernaum

Cana

Nazareth

Mediterranean Sea

Samaria

SAMARIA

PEREA

Emmaus

Jerusalem

Bethlehem

Dead Sea

JUDEA

Masada

Roman province

States controlled by the Romans

Why is Jesus known as
THE SON OF GOD?

5

PLEASE CAN YOU SHOW US A PHOTO OF GOD?

WE DON'T KNOW WHAT GOD LOOKS LIKE. NO ONE HAS SEEN GOD.

OH WELL... I WOULD HAVE LIKED TO SEE IF JESUS LOOKED LIKE HIS FATHER.

Christians believe that Jesus is true God and true man. This is the incarnation. To find out about Jesus the man, there are accounts of the people of his time, who saw, touched, and heard him. To know Jesus as the Son of God is slightly more complicated, and yet, the evidence is everywhere!

Useful words

Messiah: The Hebrew word messiah means "anointed" or chosen by God. The Jewish kings were anointed with oil. The Greek word for "anointed" is Christ.

SINCE ANCIENT TIMES

In the time of Jesus, the Jewish people were waiting for the Messiah, God's promised king, who would unite all people in peace. The Jewish prophet Micah announced that he would be born in Bethlehem, and another prophet, Isaiah, proclaimed that his mother would be a young virgin. Isaiah and the prophet Zechariah wrote that he would be mistreated, exchanged for thirty silver coins, and then put to death. Even his resurrection (being raised to life) was foretold. Christians believe that all these promises about the Messiah were fulfilled through the life, death, and resurrection of Jesus.

A DIVINE POWER

Christians believe that in addition to fulfilling the prophecies, Jesus also demonstrated that he was much more than a messenger from God. His miracles showed that he had the power and authority of God, as the Son of God. Jesus did many extraordinary things, but with no accomplice or hidden trick of a magician to explain his wonders. Through his divine power, Jesus healed sick people, multiplied loaves and fish, chased away demons, walked on water, stilled storms, and resurrected the dead.

A WORD OF WISDOM

"The Holy Spirit will come on you, and the power of the Most High will overshadow you. So the holy one to be born will be called the Son of God."
Angel Gabriel to the Virgin Mary, mother of Jesus (Luke 1:35)

JESUS REVEALS HIMSELF

In the Gospels, there are also accounts of people who realized that Jesus was the Son of God and Jesus did not deny this. For example, a woman named Martha says, "I believe that you are the Messiah, the Son of God, who is to come into the world." The disciple Peter declares, "You are the Messiah, the Son of the living God." Jesus asks him to keep this secret until he has risen.

Name: Simeon
Date: 1st century
Special event:
The Holy Spirit told him that he would not die until he had seen God's Messiah. When Mary and Joseph presented baby Jesus in the Temple of Jerusalem, Simeon immediately knew this baby was the one.

GOD SPEAKS

On two occasions in the Gospels, God declared that Jesus was his Son. These were when Jesus was baptized by John the Baptist in the river Jordan and when Jesus was transfigured (radiantly transformed). Both times, the voice of God was heard, saying, "This is my Son, whom I love; with him I am well pleased."

IN ANY CASE, HE LOOKS LIKE HIS MOTHER.

A WORD OF WISDOM

A Roman centurion stood at the foot of the cross of Jesus. He was not a believer, but he heard the last words of Jesus. "When the centurion and those with him who were guarding Jesus saw the earthquake and all that had happened, they were terrified, and exclaimed, 'Surely he was the Son of God!'"

(Matthew 27:54)

✓ TO FIND OUT ABOUT THE WRITTEN EVIDENCE,
GO TO...
13

✓ TO DISCOVER MORE ABOUT JESUS' MIRACLES,
GO TO...
18

Who is God the
HOLY SPIRIT?

6

THE HOLY SPIRIT TOOK THE FORM OF A DOVE AND DESCENDED ON JESUS.

THE HOLY SPIRIT IS THE WIND THAT PUSHES US FORWARD!

COME SPIRIT OF FIRE, COME TO SET US ABLAZE!

THIS HOLY SPIRIT COMES IN MANY DISGUISES!

Christians believe that the Spirit of God is God at work in the world. Although unseen, several images are used to represent the Holy Spirit.

POWERFUL BREATH

The Spirit of God is the breath that in the beginning was hovering over the waters. The Bible says that every living thing has the life-giving breath of the Spirit, like air that is needed to live. Or like a wind lifting a kite into the sky. The Holy Spirit is a breath that gives momentum and a desire to know God.

BURNING FIRE

The Spirit of God came like flames of fire on the first followers of Jesus. When Jesus returned to heaven, he promised to send a "Helper" to his disciples. On the day of Pentecost, they were gathered, and what seemed

like tongues of fire rested on them, filling them and enabling them to talk in many languages so that they could tell others about Jesus. Like a flaming torch, the Spirit of God shows and guides the way to God.

DOVE OF PEACE

The Spirit of God descended like a dove and rested upon Jesus at his baptism in the river Jordan. A dove is the symbol of peace. The Holy Spirit brings the peace of God into hearts, enabling the believer to show the love of God to everyone.

MYSTERIOUS...

The Holy Spirit is sometimes called Paraclete. This name means "Counsellor" in Greek. Christians believe the Spirit of God dwells within every believer, reminding them of Jesus, teaching and guiding them, comforting and protecting them, and defending them in difficult times.

DO YOU THINK IT COULD BE HIM?

AND WHAT...

are the fruit of the Spirit?

The apostle Paul in his letters to the early churches referred to the fruit of the Spirit that lives inside every believer, helping them to be more like Jesus. These "fruit" are love, joy, peace, patience, kindness, goodness, faithfulness, gentleness, and self-control.

✓ TO FIND OUT MORE ABOUT THE TRINITY GOD, GO TO...

7

✓ TO DISCOVER MORE ABOUT THE FIRST CHRISTIANS, GO TO...

8

What is the TRINITY?

1+1+1=1. This is a formula that would mystify mathematicians. But this is the mystery of the Holy Trinity. Christians believe in one God who is three persons: the Father, the Son, and the Holy Spirit. So the Trinity is like 1+1+1 = 1

Useful words

Trinity: An early Christian writer, Tertullian, invented the word "trinity" to talk about God. It combines two Latin words that mean "three" and "one".

Mystery: The Trinity is a mystery that will never be completely understood.

SEVERAL GODS

In some religions, people believe in several gods – a god for happiness, another for thunder, another for good fortune. Christians believe that there is only one God, who is the origin of all life – a loving God, who provides and cares for all that was created and has a special relationship with humankind.

GOD IN THREE PERSONS

In the second part of the Bible, the New Testament, God sends his Son, Jesus, to earth. Jesus talks about God as Father. And when Jesus returns to heaven, the Holy Spirit comes. The three persons of Father, Son, and Spirit are one and the same God.

MYSTERIOUS...

The word "Trinity" does not appear in the Bible, but this explains the set of beliefs held by Christians. Some Christians make the sign of the cross, saying the words, "In the name of the Father, Son, and Holy Spirit". This reminds them that they believe in one God in three persons.

AS ONE

If there is just one God, then why talk about three persons? Because each person of the one God loves and relates to people in a special way. God the Father loves as creator, caring and providing for all. God the Son humbled himself, becoming human and, out of love, dying to save humankind. God the Holy Spirit is God at work in the world, making known this love of God.

The Trinity
1 + 1 + 1 = 1

HE IS NOT VERY GOOD AT MATHS!

✓ TO FIND OUT ABOUT THE SON OF GOD, GO TO...

5

✓ TO DISCOVER THE SIGNS OF CHRISTIANS, GO TO...

24

Who were the
FIRST CHRISTIANS?

8

The very first Christians were Jews, like Jesus. They were the followers of Jesus. The apostles were the ones specially chosen by Jesus to be his closest disciples. They learned from Jesus and saw that he was the Messiah – the Son of God sent to save all people. However, the term "Christian" was given to them later.

FROM JEW TO GENTILE

Until the arrival of Jesus, the Jewish people believed that their faith in one God and their relationship was special to them. Jesus' message about belonging to the kingdom of God was aimed at the Jews but also welcoming to all other people. The apostles continued Jesus' work to spread the good news not only to Jews but also to the Gentiles (non-Jews).

AND WHY...

was a fish the sign of the first Christians?
The first Christians were banned from meeting and proclaiming their faith in "Jesus Christ Son of God Saviour". In Greek, the first letters of these five words form the word "ICHTHUS", which means fish. Therefore, they were able to communicate their faith secretly by drawing a fish.

THE COURAGE OF FAITH

In the beginning, Christians were just a small community meeting with the apostles. Then, they increased in number and the Jewish leaders did not like this. They arrested them and tried to stop them. Stephen became the first Christian killed for his faith in Jesus. Later, the Romans criticized the Christians for not worshipping the Roman emperor and this began the time of persecution in Rome. Despite the danger, nothing stopped the faith of these early followers of Christ, and they continued to spread the news about Jesus and his message.

MYSTERIOUS...

All Christians believe that Jesus is important to their faith, but there have been disputes that have resulted in the establishment of different churches. Believers may vary on how they practise their faith in worship and in their lives.

WE COULD HAVE SAID JESUSIANITY

Useful words

Persecuted: Badly treated and even killed for having a set of beliefs.

Catholic: In the Greek language this word means "universal". The message of Christ was spread to all people.

✓ TO FIND OUT ABOUT THE APOSTLES,
GO TO...
16

✓ TO DISCOVER ABOUT THE CHRISTIAN COMMUNITY,
GO TO...
25

What is HEAVEN LIKE?

9

WHAT ARE YOU LOOKING FOR?

HEAVEN. I WANT TO SEE WHAT IT LOOKS LIKE.

GOD IS IN HEAVEN, BUT I CAN'T FIND HIM.

Christians believe there is a heaven where God reigns in glory. Jesus spoke about his Father in heaven and, after his earthly life, Jesus returned to be with God the Father. No one knows what heaven is like, but everything is thought to be infinitely good and wonderful there. Believers hope to go there after death to be with God forever.

PERFECT HOME

Jesus often spoke about the kingdom of heaven. He described heaven as the home of God, with many rooms that he was going to prepare for those who followed him. There were angels in heaven that glorified God. He told stories about heaven being a place of incredible value like the greatest treasure, and a place full of joy and reward for faithfulness.

Useful words

Resurrection: After three days in a tomb, Jesus was raised to life. He appeared to his followers in a resurrected body, eating with his friends, before ascending to heaven. This is a central belief of Christianity.

AT THE END OF TIME

Christians believe that the resurrection of Jesus means that they can enter eternal life after death, too. At the end of time, everybody will be resurrected (raised to life) on the Day of Judgment. God will judge everyone individually. They will be raised as a spiritual body, which cannot die, and enter a new kingdom of perfection and fullness with Jesus Christ as king, glorifying God.

MYSTERIOUS...

Heaven, or paradise, is described as a place of exceptional happiness and delight. The first paradise was the Garden of Eden where Adam and Eve walked with God. Believers consider paradise to be the temporary place of blessing for those who have lived righteously during their time on earth. Catholic Christians believe in a waiting place called purgatory to prepare souls for meeting with God.

 PROFILE

Name: The sorry thief
Occupation: Criminal
Special event:
Crucified next to Jesus, he acknowledges that Jesus is the Son of God, and asks to be remembered by him. Jesus replies, "Today you will be with me in Paradise."

I'M READY TO GO TO HEAVEN!

✓ TO FIND OUT ABOUT ADAM AND EVE. GO TO...

3

✓ TO DISCOVER ABOUT THE PARABLES OF JESUS. GO TO...

19

Does God really
FORGIVE EVERYTHING?

I CONFESS THAT I HAVE DONE WRONG. I AM SORRY, AND I ASK FOR FORGIVENESS.

MAY GOD HAVE MERCY ON YOU.

IT'S GREAT! ALL MY SINS ARE FORGIVEN, EVEN THE BIG ONES THAT I DIDN'T SAY.

BUT YOU KNOW GOD SEES EVERYTHING?!

When two friends argue, sometimes they reach a point where they avoid one another. Other times, only when one friend takes the first step to say sorry, do they forgive each other. The argument is forgotten and the friendship blossoms again. Christians follow another view about forgiveness.

A FORGIVING GOD

Christians believe God created a loving, perfect world, but humans miss the mark, or sin. God loves people so much that he sent his perfect son, Jesus, to bear the sins of the world, providing a way to generously forgive again and again. God freely offers this. However, people must want to receive this from God. Jesus told a story about a reckless son, who left home with his inheritance money and went his own

way. The father waited hopefully for his son's return ready to welcome him home.

A CONDITION

In the Gospels in the Bible, Jesus taught that to receive God's forgiveness, people must also forgive those who have wronged them – even if the person wrongs them again and again or even if they are not sorry. Believers must release others from blame and trust God for justice, leaving the situation completely in God's merciful hands.

A WORD OF WISDOM

"Then Peter came to Jesus and asked, 'Lord, how many times shall I forgive my brother or sister who sins against me? Up to seven times?' Jesus answered, 'I tell you, not seven times, but seventy-seven times.'"

(Matthew 18:21–22)

HE CAN'T SEE ME, HERE!

Useful words

Mercy: Loving compassion and kindness towards those in need, especially shown in forgiveness.

✓ TO FIND OUT MORE ABOUT JESUS' TEACHINGS, GO TO…
17

✓ TO DISCOVER IF GOD IS LOVE, GO TO…
11

Investigation Report

Name of witness:
Saint Paul

Profession:
Apostle of Jesus Christ

You are here today as a witness of God's mercy. Why?
I was a great sinner and yet God has forgiven me. He even chose me to go and tell others about Jesus as his apostle.

What did you do wrong?
I was known for persecuting the first followers of Jesus. I was chasing these men and women, dragging them from their homes and throwing them into jail.

What happened to change your life around?
On the way from Jerusalem to Damascus, the resurrected Jesus appeared to me. I realized that he was the Messiah, the Son of God. Jesus stopped me from persecuting his followers, forgave me, and gave me a mission to spread his good news. I was overwhelmed.

How are you living now?
It is not about me anymore. Christ lives in me.

Do you have any message to others?
Let yourself be reconciled with God. Accept his forgiveness and his love. And forgive those who hurt you.

Why do believers say that
GOD IS LOVE?

11

A king reigns. A chief commands. A master orders. A lord dominates. And a dad… loves. Jesus does not tell his followers to call God "Majesty", "Master" or "Lord" but invites them to say, "Our Father". God loves as a father with infinite love.

LOVED FOREVER

A father loves his children from before their birth and helps them grow throughout their lives. He feeds them and supports them. Christians believe that God loves as a father, creating each person and knowing each of us from the time we were in our mother's womb. God gave breath and life, and provided for us.

"See what great love the Father has lavished on us, that we should be called children of God! And that is what we are!"

(1 John 3:1)

LOVED TO BRING JOY

Christians see themselves as children of God. God as Father encourages and supports his children to help them make good choices, sending the Holy Spirit to guide them in their lives and their faith. Like a father, God blesses and wishes joy for all his children, which is greater than anyone could imagine.

LOVED TO THE END

Christians believe that, like a loving father, God forgives and guides them through their mistakes. God rejoices with all people in moments of joy and supports and comforts them in difficult times. Even more wonderful is that God gives his most precious gift, his Son, to save all people from being separated from him by sin and death.

✓ TO FIND OUT GOD'S PLAN FOR HUMANS,
GO TO…
27

✓ TO DISCOVER MORE ABOUT GOD THE SPIRIT,
GO TO…
6

Why is the Bible called
THE WORD OF GOD?

The Bible is a collection of sixty-six books. As in any library, the books were written by different people. It was not written by God resting on a cloud, writing with a beautiful feather. Instead, Christians believe that God inspired the words of the authors.

ANCIENT WORDS

The Bible was written by several people, writing over a period of hundreds of years. The first Bible stories were told and passed down before being written on clay tablets and then on papyrus scrolls. Historians think that the first written accounts of the Bible date back to about 1,000 years before Jesus and the last ones were written about 100 years after his birth.

Useful words

Old Testament: The word "testament" means "covenant" (agreement). The Old Testament is the story of the covenant made between God and the Hebrew people.

New Testament: In sending his Son, Jesus, to earth, God made a new agreement with all people. This is the story found in this section of the Bible.

INSPIRED WORDS

The Bible is said to be the Word of God because those who wrote the texts were inspired by God. The authors used their own words and reflected on what they saw or heard to convey who God is. But these words were inspired by the Spirit of God, so their text is full of faith and helps people to understand God. Through the Bible, Christians believe God reveals who he is, how he acts in our lives, and how much he loves us.

AND WHY...

are there small numbers all over the Bible?
The Bible is divided into chapters and verses to help people find their way around the books. When looking for a text in the Bible, this is given with a few letters to indicate the name of the book (for example "Gen" for the book of Genesis), then the chapter number followed by a comma or a colon and then the verse reference. A verse refers to the little passages or phrases within each chapter.

LIVING WORDS

The Bible is called the living Word of God because the text is still applicable to people who live today. When speaking to someone, you never know which way the conversation will lead, for this depends on you and the person you are speaking with. Reading the Bible is as if God is talking to the reader. The reader never knows what God is going to say on the day that the Bible is opened. Sometimes, readers may be very familiar with the text, but on a particular day, they may discover a new meaning as God inspires them.

A LIBRARY

The Bible is not usually read like a normal book, starting at the beginning and finishing at the end. Some texts are trickier to read than others and this may be discouraging. Instead, readers may read and study the individual books. Readers will quickly discover that there are different styles of writing in the Bible, from poems and love stories, words of wisdom and songs, to history, laws, and letters.

 PROFILE

Name: Saint Jerome
Dates: 347-420
Work:
Jerome was a Latin priest and scholar. He translated the entire Bible into Latin, which was the common language at the time. His work is often called the Vulgate, which means the Bible for everyone.

GOD IS VERY TALKATIVE!

✓ TO FIND OUT WHO WROTE THE GOSPELS, GO TO...

14

✓ TO DISCOVER IF THE BIBLE IS HISTORICALLY TRUE, GO TO...

13

Is the Bible HISTORICALLY ACCURATE?

Aquarium

This one?

NOT BIG ENOUGH!

I'M LOOKING FOR THE BIG FISH THAT COULD HAVE SWALLOWED JONAH AND THEN SPAT HIM OUT ON THE BEACH.

SECURITY

The Bible is a mixture of different writing styles. In the first section, the Old Testament, some books tell the stories of the Israelites, and others contain their laws or words of wisdom or prophecy. The stories are written to teach people a truth about God.

WORDS AND IMAGES

The writers of the Bible used a variety of narrative techniques, or genres, that were often fashionable in their time or matched their writing talent. There are tales of characters who may not have existed, and poems or songs. The last book of the Bible, Revelation, even reads like a science fiction story, although it is an account of a vision. The different styles of writing correspond to the time and different authors, but this does not take anything from the truth of the message and its relevance today.

A WORD OF WISDOM

"Many have undertaken to draw up an account of the things that have been fulfilled among us, just as they were handed down to us by those who from the first were eyewitnesses and servants of the word. With this in mind, since I myself have carefully investigated everything from the beginning, I too decided to write an orderly account for you, most excellent Theophilus, so that you may know the certainty of the things you have been taught."

Luke Chapter 1:1-4

ONE TRUTH

In the Bible there are historical accounts that describe events that took place. There are also the Gospels, which are the accounts of the life of Jesus, and the letters of the first Christians, encouraging other believers. These texts teach truth about God, allowing the reader to get to know and love God more. The Bible is a library of books, but all are about the same subject: God. By reading each of the books of the Bible, readers discover one great truth: God has a special relationship with humans and a great loving plan full of promises and hopes from the beginning to the end of time.

MYSTERIOUS...

The Bible is not a science book, but it is helpful to study the texts in the context of how people lived and what was happening in their lives. Knowing what was happening when the Bible passages were written can help to add understanding and profound meaning to the message.

IN YOUR OPINION, HOW TALL WAS GOLIATH?

✓ TO FIND OUT ABOUT THE MESSAGES IN THE BIBLE, GO TO...

19

✓ TO DISCOVER WHO IS SPEAKING THROUGH THE BIBLE, GO TO...

12

Who wrote
THE GOSPELS?

14

Did you know that the three musketeers were really four? Their names were Athos, Porthos, Aramis, and d'Artagnan. They were four men with the same motto: "One for all and all for one". The four evangelists – the name given to those who wrote about the life of Jesus in the Bible – were: Matthew, Mark, Luke, and John. They could have that same motto: "ONE for all and all for ONE". This "ONE" is Jesus!

ONE FOR ALL

Christians believe that Jesus came for all people. Men, women, children. The rich and the poor. The sick and the healthy. The Jewish people and the Gentiles (non-Jewish). To share Christ's message with all of humanity, each evangelist wrote their account aimed at a different audience. For example, Matthew's Gospel was mainly aimed at the Jewish people. He often referred to passages in the Old Testament, which has the same content as the Jewish holy books, to show how Jesus fulfilled their prophecies. Mark's Gospel was written for the persecuted Christians in Rome to support them in their faith. Each witness account tells about Jesus' life, his character, and his impact on those he met.

Useful words

Gospel: This comes from a Greek word meaning "good news".

ALL FOR ONE

The four evangelists wrote their accounts for the glory of one: Jesus! The Gospels are all a bit different, but this helps to provide different aspects of who Jesus was. The four accounts complement each other. Some episodes of Jesus' life are just in one Gospel; for example, the foot washing at the Last Supper is only written by John. Other events are told differently according to what has particularly affected the writer. The Gospels taken together form a whole that helps

MYSTERIOUS...

Of the four evangelists, only two knew Jesus. Matthew and John were his apostles. Mark was a friend of the apostles Peter and Paul. Luke was a Syrian doctor. Mark's Gospel is the oldest, written around sixty to seventy years after the birth of Jesus. Matthew's and Luke's Gospels date from eighty to ninety years after, and John's Gospel dates from ninety to one hundred years after.

readers to understand Jesus and his message. They provide the groundwork of the Christian faith.

I WONDER WHAT A DOCTOR THOUGHT ABOUT JESUS' MIRACLES?

AND WHY...

are different Gospels read in church services?
For some church groups, a different Gospel is read through each year. One year might be devoted to the whole of the Matthew's Gospel; the following year, Mark's Gospel, and finally, Luke's Gospel. The Gospel of John is used for important festivals.

✓ TO FIND OUT ABOUT THE MIRACLES OF JESUS, GO TO...
18

✓ TO DISCOVER WHO INSPIRED THE EVANGELISTS, GO TO...
12

Was Jesus born at MIDNIGHT ON 25 DECEMBER?

15

I WONDER WHAT DATE IS ON THE BIRTH CERTIFICATE OF JESUS?

SO WHAT?

DO YOU THINK IT SAYS 25 DECEMBER ?

OF COURSE! THAT IS CHRISTMAS DAY!

A birth certificate records the place, date, and time of birth. The information is also kept in registers in the town of birth. In the time of Jesus, this was not done, so it is impossible to know exactly the date and time of his birth.

AN ESTIMATE

The precise date of Jesus' birth is not known; however, historians have been able to calculate more or less the year of his birth from historical accounts. They refer to King Herod's reign and work back from an account stating when Jesus began preaching. The early Christians celebrated his birth on 6 January, at the same time as the visit of the Magi, his baptism, and the wedding at Cana. In 353, Christians decided to separate these events and chose 25 December for celebrating his birth. Why this date?

25 DECEMBER

A SYMBOLIC DATE

Some non-Christian people celebrated the winter solstice on 25 December. Until that time, days get shorter and nights are longer. After this time, days start getting longer again, with more light. The Bible says, "the people living in darkness have seen a great light". The time of Jesus symbolizes the end of night and the return of day, the defeat of darkness and evil. At the birth of Jesus, Christians also celebrate the victory of God's light and love.

AND WHY...

was Jesus born in a crib?
Originally, the word "crib" meant the animal feeder or manger where Mary laid baby Jesus. Gradually, the word was used to refer to the barn where Mary and Joseph stayed as there was no room in any inns in Bethlehem. Jesus had a humble birth.

IF JESUS WASN'T BORN AT CHRISTMAS, THEN HE MUST RECEIVE GIFTS TWICE!

Useful words

Christmas: The word literally means "Christ's Mass", a time for reflection about the beginning of the Christian faith.

✓ TO FIND OUT WHY JESUS IS CALLED THE SON OF GOD, GO TO...
5

✓ TO DISCOVER ABOUT JESUS' DEATH, GO TO...
20

The Christian Year

Throughout the year, Christians celebrate important events in the life of Jesus. This calendar is called the liturgical year.

ATTENTION!

The liturgical year does not begin on January 1 but on the first Sunday of Advent, a four-week period of preparation for Jesus' birth.

Each period corresponds with a colour for the vestments (clothing) of the priests or ministers and the coverings in church.

- ● Ordinary time
- ○ Major festivals
- ● Sign of penitence
- ● Holy Spirit or the death of Jesus

Didn't Jesus have
UNUSUAL FRIENDS?

THOMAS, WOULD YOU LIKE TO BECOME A FRIEND OF JESUS?

I WILL BUT...

I'M NOT SURE THAT HE WILL WANT ME.

WHY'S THAT?

WELL, I'M NOT ILL, A DISABLED PERSON, OR A THIEF.

At first glance, Jesus chooses surprising friends, who were the outcasts of society. These included thieves, those with leprosy, prostitutes, those possessed by demons, and the unpopular tax collectors. But Jesus welcomed everyone.

Useful words

Apostle: In Greek, this word means "sent". Jesus sent his chosen apostles on a mission to go and proclaim the good news to the world.

Disciple: A person who receives teaching from a master and follows his example.

THE WEAK

The Gospels are full of stories about the people that Jesus met and the impact he had on their lives. These people had their lives changed when they followed Jesus and became his friend. They were the poor and the weak, those who were sick, and those who had been rejected by Jewish society for doing things wrong. Jesus said he had come "to proclaim good news to the poor, freedom for the prisoners, recovery of sight for the blind and set the oppressed free". He wanted to touch their hearts with the love of God.

PROFILES OF THE APOSTLES

◆ ◆ ◆

Name: Simon, son of John or Jonah

Nickname: Peter or Cephas

Occupation: fisherman; Jesus entrusted him with his Church.

Name: Andrew

Occupation: fisherman; disciple of John the Baptist; first apostle to follow Jesus with his brother Simon Peter.

Name: James, son of Zebedee

Nickname: Elder

Occupation: fisherman, like his brother John.

Name: John, son of Zebedee

Nickname: Son of thunder, brother of James

Occupation: fisherman; known as the disciple that Jesus loved, who followed him to the cross; author of the fourth Gospel.

Name: Philip

Occupation: disciple of John the Baptist; invited Nathanael to follow Jesus.

Name: Bartholomew

Nickname: Nathanael.

Name: Matthew

Nickname: Levi

Occupation: tax collector; author of the first Gospel in the Bible.

Name: Thomas

Nickname: Didymus (Twin); refused to believe the resurrection of Jesus; spread the good news to India.

Name: James, son of Alphaeus

Nickname: Younger.

Name: Simon

Nickname: Zealot, as strongly against the occupation of the Romans.

Name: Jude

Nickname: Judas, son of James or Thaddeus.

Name: Judas

Nickname: Iscariot; the treasurer of the group of apostles and the one who betrayed Jesus. He was replaced by Matthias.

 The palm branch signifies the apostles that died as martyrs.

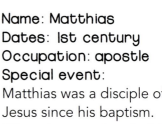
These men and women – the outcasts of society – best understood Jesus and his message. In contrast to the rich young man who would like to follow Jesus but doesn't want to leave his fortune behind, the poor and weak had nothing, and Jesus' message was full of hope for them. Their lives were transformed.

ORDINARY MEN

Jesus' closest friends, the apostles, are not extraordinary. They are neither the cleverest, the richest, the youngest, nor the bravest. They did not hold important positions in society and were not very successful. The apostles were simple men with flaws and a variety of qualities. This shows that even the weakest person is welcome to follow and love Jesus, is valued by Jesus, and can do great things in the name of Jesus.

AND I'M NOT A GOOD FISHERMAN, EITHER...

✓ TO FIND OUT WHAT JESUS' MESSAGE WAS, GO TO...

19

✓ TO DISCOVER MORE ABOUT THE GOSPELS, GO TO...

14

What were Jesus' COMMANDMENTS?

NICE DOG!

THOMAS, WHAT ARE YOU DOING?

Attention Guard Dog

I'M JUST PRACTISING WHAT JESUS SAID: "LOVE YOUR ENEMIES."

In the Old Testament, the Jewish people received ten commandments from God. When asked which was the greatest commandment, Jesus replied with just two that summarized them: "Love the Lord your God with all your heart, soul and mind" and "Love others as you do yourself." This second command went further…

LOVE YOUR ENEMIES

It is easy for people to love those who like them and whom they get along well with. However, it is harder for people to love those who annoy or criticize them or even hurt them. Jesus invited everyone to love those people, too. He said to his disciples, "Love your enemies." This seems impossible, but Jesus knows his followers are capable of doing what seems difficult. He did this himself. He showed how to look at our enemies full of love, to find the good in them, to forgive them completely, and to be peacemakers.

A MODEL OF LOVE

Jesus said, "As I have loved you, so you must love one another." Jesus showed that it is in the small as well as the large gestures that people can show love to others. He showed his followers how to forgive, to serve others, and to be compassionate and kind. This was only possible by trusting in and knowing the love of God.

A WORD OF WISDOM

"Love is patient, love is kind. It does not envy, it does not boast, it is not proud. It does not dishonour others, it is not self-seeking, it is not easily angered, it keeps no record of wrongs."
Saint Paul's letter to the Church of Corinth (1 Corinthians 13:4–5)

IT'S EASIER WITH A BONE!

✓ TO FIND OUT ABOUT THE GOD OF LOVE,
GO TO...
11

✓ TO DISCOVER IF JESUS REALLY DID MIRACLES,
GO TO...
18

Did Jesus really
DO MIRACLES?

18

There were plenty of witnesses to Jesus' miracles. Over five thousand men, women, and children were fed with just five loaves and two fish. When Jesus healed the lame man, there were so many people in the house that his friends lowered him through the roof to reach Jesus. These wonders showed God's power at work.

WAS JESUS A SUPERHERO?

Jesus walked on water and calmed a storm by ordering the wind to be quiet. He raised his friend Lazarus from the dead after several days in a tomb. He healed the servant of a Roman centurion without even going to his house. Jesus demonstrated a power much stronger than any superhero's. The miracles of Jesus show his great love for people, his great capacity for forgiveness, and God's power and authority over everything that was created.

Useful words

Miracle: An inexplicable event. This word is formed from two Latin words that mean "object of wonder".

EXTRAVAGANT LOVE

At the wedding of Cana, Jesus turned water into wine that was even better than that provided by the groom. The miraculous catch of fish was so abundant that the nets were at breaking point. After the feeding of the five thousand, there were twelve baskets of food left over. Not only does Jesus heal those who are sick, but he forgives them completely. Jesus demonstrated the abundance of God's love for humankind, which is more than believers can hope and imagine.

MYSTERIOUS...

Loving like Jesus enables believers to do amazing things: restore peace, bring joy, comfort, and healing. These miracles may not be spectacular, but they show God's love for the world.

WHAT DO YOU THINK JESUS' COSTUME LOOKED LIKE WHEN HE WAS WALKING ON WATER?

✓ TO FIND OUT ABOUT WHO JESUS IS. GO TO...
5

✓ TO DISCOVER MORE ABOUT THE LOVE OF GOD. 0 TO...
11

ARE PARABLES
CODED MESSAGES?

19

A coded message has its information scrambled into a set of letters or symbols so that only the people with the code can read it. This is designed to minimize the number of people who can decipher it. A parable works in completely the opposite way. Jesus told stories to simplify a message so as many people as possible could understand its meaning.

DECODING A MESSAGE

Jesus' parables work a bit like TV shows where complicated signals are transformed into a picture that anyone can look at. Jesus provided an image of the message that he wanted to share with people. He told stories that people could understand to help explain what God was like and what the kingdom of God was like, and how to love one another.

STORIES ABOUT EVERYDAY LIFE

In the time of Jesus, many people were farmers and shepherds, and there were rich and poor. Jesus used familiar situations and subjects in his stories, such as sowing seeds, losing sheep, vineyards, and servants. The parable of the good Samaritan was about showing kindness even to enemies, as the Jewish people did not like those from the nearby region of Samaria. A few of the parables are explained in the Gospels, but many are left for the listener to consider and understand the meaning for themselves.

MYSTERIOUS...

There are about forty parables in the Gospels. Some are told in several Gospels, but most can be found in Luke's Gospel. John's Gospel uses images on two occasions and are not called parables.

FOR TODAY

The parables of Jesus continue to help readers of the Bible understand the message that Jesus taught. Although the situation has changed, the stories still "speak" to people and relate to their lives.

ARE YOU STILL LOOKING?

YES, JESUS SAID, "SEEK AND YOU WILL FIND."

✓ TO FIND OUT MORE ABOUT THE TEXTS IN THE BIBLE,
GO TO...
13

✓ TO DISCOVER THE MESSAGE OF JESUS,
GO TO...
17

What proves that Jesus REALLY DIED?

On the first Easter, the apostles claimed that Jesus rose from the dead. The Jewish people and the Romans thought that this was impossible. They thought that the apostles lied or made everything look as if Jesus were resurrected; maybe Jesus had not really died but just passed out on the cross. The resurrection of Jesus is incredible, so many seek an explanation.

DEATH ON THE CROSS

Being crucified was a slow, painful way to die. It was the Romans' punishment for criminals. After several hours, if the person was still not dead, the Roman soldiers broke their legs to quicken the death. No prisoners escaped. After such treatment, Jesus was truly dead, and many witnesses saw this: the crowd, the chief priests, and the soldiers. It was not necessary for the soldiers to break Jesus' legs, as he had already died.

Useful words

Salvation: The act of God saving humans made possible through the death and resurrection of Jesus.

AND RESURRECTED!

The Jewish prophets in the Old Testament wrote about the death of the Messiah. Jesus had also told his closest friends, the apostles, what would happen to him. Although he was innocent, he was to die on a cross like a criminal, but three days later his death took on a whole new meaning. He was resurrected and appeared to many people over the next forty days. Christians believe that Jesus died on the cross as an act of incredible sacrifice and love for all people. He took on the sins of all people to save them, releasing them from sin and overcoming death. This act of salvation brought them back into a new relationship with God.

AND WHY...

did soldiers pierce Jesus' side if he was already dead?

As the Jewish Sabbath (day of rest) was soon to begin, the soldiers had to hasten the death of those crucified. A soldier pierced Jesus' side with a spear to check that he was dead. He was, so they did not break the bones in his legs. This fulfilled prophecies found in the Old Testament.

ARE YOU SURE WE MUST WAIT ANOTHER THREE DAYS?

BAKERY

✓ TO FIND OUT WHY GOD LET HIS SON BE KILLED.
GO TO...
11

✓ TO DISCOVER MORE ABOUT GOD'S FORGIVENESS.
GO TO...
10

What happens during Holy Week?

The last week of Lent, the one before Easter, is called Holy Week. These are the events remembered...

PALM SUNDAY

The event: Jesus enters Jerusalem riding on a donkey. The crowd cheers and waves palm branches, shouting, "Blessed is the king who comes in the name of the Lord! Hosanna in the highest heaven!"

MAUNDY THURSDAY

The event: Jesus eats his last meal with his apostles. During the meal he washes their feet to show them how to serve one another. He then takes bread and wine, gives thanks to God, and asks them to remember him when they eat and drink. He breaks the bread, saying, "This is my body", and he passes around the cup, saying, "This is my blood poured out for the forgiveness of sins."

FROM THURSDAY NIGHT TO GOOD FRIDAY

The event: Jesus prays in a garden of olive trees, Gethsemane. A large crowd of temple guards comes led by the disciple Judas, who betrays Jesus with a kiss. Jesus is arrested and taken to the house of the high priest.

GOOD FRIDAY

The event: Jesus is tried before the Jewish council, King Herod, and the Roman governor Pontius Pilate and sentenced to death. He carries his cross to Calgary and is crucified. There is darkness across the land. Jesus dies at 3 p.m., the earth shakes, and the Temple curtain is torn in two. Jesus' body is laid in a tomb and a large stone rolled in front.

NIGHT OF SATURDAY TO SUNDAY

The event: Jesus rises from the dead, the earth shakes, and the stone in front of the tomb is rolled away. Some women bring spices to the tomb, but angels appear to them and say, "Why do you look for the living among the dead? He is not here; he has risen!"

21 WERE THE APOSTLES cowards?

When Jesus was arrested, his friends fled. Only Peter followed him to the house of the high priest, but then he denied knowing Jesus three times. The disciples were scared and felt in danger of being arrested, too. They were probably confused as well, for they thought that Jesus was the Messiah sent by God to deliver them from the Romans, not to die on a cross like a criminal. They did not understand, even though Jesus had told them what to expect.

A COUNSELLOR

When Jesus was with the apostles, they were confident, but when he was no longer with them, they were afraid. After his resurrection, Jesus appeared and ate with them many times. He forgave Peter for denying him and asked him to lead his Church. Jesus knew that when he returned to heaven to join his Father, they would need a Helper. He sent them out to make disciples, baptize, and tell others about his teaching, but he told them to wait until they received the Holy Spirit.

Useful words

Pentecost: Fifty days after Easter, Jesus sent the Holy Spirit to his apostles. In Greek, the fiftieth day is said to be pentekoste hemera.

MYSTERIOUS...

After receiving the Holy Spirit at Pentecost, the apostles started talking in many languages. The crowd was amazed to hear these simple men speak in their language so that they could understand what they were saying about Jesus. The whole world was now able to hear about Jesus' message. This was the birth of the Church.

A HOLY FORCE

On the day of Pentecost, the apostles received the Holy Spirit and were filled with strength and courage. They no longer stayed hidden but went out into the streets to tell others about Jesus Christ. Although they were imprisoned, their lives were threatened, and they faced many difficulties, they were not afraid. They were ready to bear witness to the good news of Jesus, and some even died for their beliefs.

HOW MANY LANGUAGES DID YOU SPEAK AT YOUR BAPTISM?

✓ TO FIND OUT ABOUT THE FIRST CHRISTIANS, GO TO...
8

✓ TO DISCOVER MORE ABOUT THE HOLY SPIRIT, GO TO...
6

Who invented PRAYER?

At school, children may be asked to write a poem to their parents or carers. They may not be perfect, but no doubt the receiver will be very touched by the words. It does not matter about the phrases or vocabulary used, but what matters is the love that is put into the words.

PRAYER OF THE HEART

A prayer is a conversation of love, friendship, and praise to God. Christians believe that prayer is a two-way conversation, so believers make time to be still and listen, too. Sometimes the words do not come easily, so there are plenty of prayers that can be read or learned to use instead. These prayers may have been said hundreds of years ago, while others only yesterday. Prayers have been written by people all over the world, reminding believers that everyone can pray, and God is present everywhere.

A WORD OF WISDOM

"May the grace of our Lord Jesus Christ, and the love of God, and the fellowship of the Holy Spirit be with us all now and evermore. Amen."

The Grace prayer based on Paul's prayer at the end of 2 Corinthians 13:14

PRAYING WITH THE BIBLE

There are many prayers found in the Bible. The best-known ones are found in the book of Psalms. There are ones that praise and celebrate, and others that express feelings, such as joy, sadness, and despair. Christians also use passages from the Bible to reflect upon and pause for a while with God and listen.

THE LORD'S PRAYER

Among all the passages of the Bible, there is one that Jesus taught his followers. The prayer is called "Our Father" or "the Lord's Prayer". It brings together everything that Christians should do when they pray: offer thanks and praise to God; say sorry; and ask for forgiveness.

LET'S SAY, "OUR FATHER"?

✓ TO FIND OUT HOW GOD ANSWERS PRAYERS, GO TO…

23

✓ TO DISCOVER MORE ABOUT THE TRINITY, GO TO…

7

THE LORD'S PRAYER

The "Our Father" is the perfect prayer that Jesus taught his followers. There is plenty to reflect on as the words are recited.

OUR FATHER
Jesus invites his followers to speak to God as "Dad" and reflect on having a God who loves them.

WHO IS IN HEAVEN
Heaven is where God is but this is not far away; instead, God sees and watches over everything.

HOLY IS YOUR NAME
This phrase gives praise and thanks to God, reflecting on God's greatness and glory.

MAY YOUR KINGDOM COME
Jesus spoke about the kingdom of God being within or among those who believe, changing and working in people's hearts to bring peace and love for all.

LET YOUR WILL BE DONE ON EARTH AS IN HEAVEN
This phrase reinforces the desire to trust and obey God and be aware of God working in the world for the best for all people.

GIVE US TODAY OUR DAILY BREAD
Jesus reminds believers that God lovingly provides everything they need, so they do not have to worry.

FORGIVE US OUR SINS
This phrase is about admitting wrongs, saying sorry, and asking to be forgiven. Christians believe God has great love and compassion for humans and offers forgiveness through Jesus Christ.

AS WE ALSO FORGIVE THOSE WHO HAVE OFFENDED US
Jesus teaches that his followers must forgive others to receive forgiveness from God.

AND LEAD US NOT INTO TEMPTATION
This phrase emphasizes that God helps in the fight against doing wrong, and to ask for this help.

BUT DELIVER US FROM EVIL
Christians believe that God sent Jesus to die and rise again to defeat evil and death, saving all people.

AMEN
This word means "so be it" and Christians use this to end prayers, affirming that they are committed to everything that has been said.

23 How does God ANSWER PRAYERS?

GOD
PARADISE
TO HEAVEN

↑ ALL DESTINATIONS

A WEEK LATER

STILL NOTHING FOR ME?

NO.

THOMAS

IT'S MYSTERIOUS. THE PRIEST SAID GOD ALWAYS ANSWERS.

Christians believe God's response to prayers often does not look like the replies usually received. God does not speak directly, or write, or call on a phone. God is unlikely to send an angel as a messenger. God answers in a subtle way.

AN UNEXPECTED ANSWER

For Christians, when they pray and ask God for things, they may have an idea about how God might answer them. For example, a student may pray that everything goes well at school, hoping to be successful. God instead may give a friend to the student, for a good friendship is more important than a good grade. Maybe someone prays for a sick person, asking God to heal them. Instead, God may send people to provide support and kindness, because this patient needs to feel loved. God knows what is best and most needed for every person.

"Ask and it will be given to you; seek and you will find; knock and the door will be opened to you."

Gospel of Matthew 7:7

MYSTERIOUS...

For Christians in many situations, patience is needed before God is seen to have answered their prayers. But God is at work continuously, acting in people's lives and putting in place the best outcome. Christians believe there is no such thing as chance but it's all part of God's plan for their lives.

SEEING GOD AT WORK

Sometimes God answers exactly as the person who prayed hoped, and then they clearly see their prayer answered. For example, a student asks to settle well in a new school, and from the very first day, several students come over to them. The student thanks God! But other times, seeing God answer prayer is harder. This takes time and an attentive heart, open to discover the presence of God even in the smallest details, such as in a conversation or a situation.

DO YOU THINK THIS IS GOD'S ANSWER?

THOMAS

COME TO CHURCH

✓ TO FIND OUT ABOUT PRAYER, GO TO...

22

✓ TO DISCOVER WHAT GOD WANTS FOR PEOPLE, GO TO...

27

What are the
SIGNS OF CHRISTIANS?

24

PHARMACY

WELL, I DIDN'T KNOW THE PHARMACIST WAS A CHRISTIAN.

When two motorcycles pass each other on a road, the riders often greet each other with a V sign for victory, repeating the gesture used by world famous motorcycle champions. This "wave" is a way of showing that they belong to the same community of bikers. When two Christians greet each other, there is no sign used, but there are signs and symbols used at other times.

A SIGN OF FAITH

Many Christians all over the world, and whatever their language, make the sign of the cross. This is a way of declaring their faith. Their hand traces the sign of the cross, saying the words, "I believe in the Father, Son, and Holy Spirit." They also declare that Jesus died and rose again to save the world from sin. This simple hand gesture powerfully declares their faith.

A WORD OF WISDOM

"For God so loved the world that he gave his one and only Son, that whoever believes in him shall not perish but have eternal life. For God did not send his Son into the world to condemn the world, but to save the world through him."

Gospel of John 3:16–17

MYSTERIOUS...

The sign of the cross begins at the forehead and goes down to the stomach, just like God's love descends on all people. Then, the cross sign stretches horizontally, from the left to the right, because the love of God that fills a person is then shared with others everywhere.

A SIGN OF LOVE

The cross is the main symbol of Christianity. It may seem like a sign of torture and death, but it is a sign of great love and freedom for Christians. They believe that Jesus died on the cross as an act of incredible sacrifice and love for all people. He took on the sins of all people to save them, releasing them from sin and overcoming death. This act of salvation brought them back into a new relationship with God so that they can receive eternal life. A cross showing Jesus is called a crucifix and reminds the believer that Jesus died for them. An empty cross reminds the believer that Jesus rose again, defeating death to offer eternal life.

FISHERMAN OR CHRISTIAN?

✓ TO FIND OUT IF JESUS REALLY DIED ON THE CROSS, GO TO...

20

✓ TO DISCOVER ABOUT GOD AS FATHER, SON, AND HOLY SPIRIT, GO TO...

7

What is the difference between the church

AND THE CHURCH?

The Church is made of living stones: YOU!

DIY STORE

BRICKS

BLOCKS

WHERE DO I FIND THE LIVING STONES?

CEMENT

PROMO

What difference is there between the church and the Church? Look closer and there is a capital letter in one. Capital letters are used for proper nouns, which includes the name of a person. The Church with a capital letter is used for the name of a gathering of people. The church with a lower-case letter is the building in which Christians gather.

THE FAMILY OF GOD

Jesus is the founder of the Church. The Church is all Christians everywhere and through all time. As the children of God, Christians are a great big family of believers. As in a family, the Church is made up of a great diversity of people. Every one is unique and precious in the eyes of God.

Useful words

Cathedral: The church where the "seat" of a bishop, who oversees a diocese, or large group of churches in an area, is located.

Basilica: A church with special importance because it was built on a holy site.

A WORD OF WISDOM

"In him the whole building is joined together and rises to become a holy temple in the Lord."

Saint Paul's letter to the Church of Ephesus (Ephesians 2:21)

THE HOUSE OF GOD

The idea of the house of God comes from when the Israelites wandered in the wilderness after leaving Egypt. They set up a Tabernacle, a holy tent, which was where God's presence lived among them. Now the house of God has become the family of believers themselves, because the Holy Spirit lives within and among them. Jesus is the cornerstone – the first one laid; the apostles are the foundation stones on which the living stones – the people – of the Church are built.

✓ TO FIND OUT ABOUT THE HOLY SPIRIT,
GO TO...

6

✓ TO DISCOVER THE STORIES OF THE FIRST CHRISTIANS,
GO TO...

8

PLAN OF A CHURCH

Over time, the building where members of the Church gathered was called a church as well. Some churches have a cross-shape plan as a reminder of the cross of Jesus and the beliefs of the faith.

◆ ◆

AN EXAMPLE OF A TRADITIONAL CHURCH PLAN

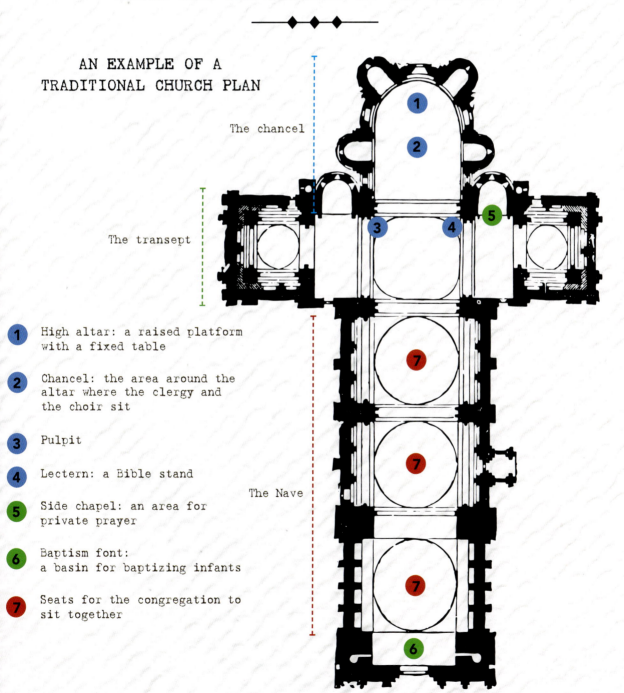

The chancel

The transept

The Nave

1. High altar: a raised platform with a fixed table

2. Chancel: the area around the altar where the clergy and the choir sit

3. Pulpit

4. Lectern: a Bible stand

5. Side chapel: an area for private prayer

6. Baptism font: a basin for baptizing infants

7. Seats for the congregation to sit together

How is Christianity different TO OTHER RELIGIONS?

A religion is a set of beliefs in an unseen higher power and the practices that believers follow. There are many religions around the world, with Christianity having the most believers. Leaders of the major world religions meet regularly. They do not discuss who has the "right" religion but instead they talk about the best way to all agree about concerns in the world.

GOD MADE KNOWN

Religious leaders think that theirs is the right religion and so do believers of every religion. Christians believe that they have the only faith in which God has made himself known, in the person of Jesus. God came down from heaven, became man, and walked among the people, but with divine power and wisdom, showing them who God is and what God can do.

REJOICE

Christians rejoice in having a God who came directly to them, to find and talk to them. They marvel at God's love for all people, even to the point of giving his life to die on a cross to save the world from evil. No one before Jesus or after him has spoken so much about love and taught people so much about how to love each other.

MYSTERIOUS...

Christianity is the only religion where followers believe their founder, Jesus Christ, came back to life. There is no grave to visit.

A WORD OF WISDOM

"See how they love each other!" Tertullian, one of the first Christian writers, reports the words of non-believers when they watched Christians

WORDS AND DEEDS

Because Christians feel loved and valued by God, they are eager to share and show this love to others as Jesus told them to do. The Spirit of God provides the strength and guidance to do this. They show their faith through words and actions, particularly reaching out to the poor, those who are in need and suffering, and those who are turned away by others. By reflecting Christ-like attitudes, love, and joy, they hope that others will want to get to know their God, too.

BUT HERE, YOU NEED TO CHOOSE?

London
Oxford
Cardiff
Glasgow
Lands End

✓ TO FIND OUT MORE ABOUT JESUS, GO TO...

4

✓ TO DISCOVER THE UNUSUAL FRIENDS OF JESUS, GO TO...

16

27 What does GOD WANT FOR PEOPLE?

What would a loving father wish for each of his children? A house? Good health? Friends? A successful business? A big family? Probably all this and much more. He would like his children to never be sad, or to never have bad things happen to them. God's plans for his children are even greater than this.

BLESSINGS

Christians believe that God loves all people like a doting father and seeks a special loving relationship with his children. Even from the womb, God knows everything about his children, generously pouring out an abundance of blessings for their happiness. God's plan is to fulfil his children's spiritual potential to the full, and God does this by his outpouring of love, compassion, and provision.

ALWAYS WITH US

Christians believe that not everything goes according to God's plan, because God created his children with freedom to choose. Sometimes bad choices are made, and lives go off course. Thankfully, even when a wrong path has been taken, God is always there, and God manages to do something good in the situation to guide them back.

A WORD OF WISDOM

"Blessed are the pure in heart,
for they will see God.
Blessed are the peacemakers,
...for they will be called children
of God."

From Jesus' Sermon on
the Mount (Matthew 5:8–9)

THE TRUST OF LOVE

For Christians, the only thing that God asks of them for their happiness to be complete is for their love and trust. A little child taking her first steps dares to run only because she knows her dad will reach out his arms and not let her fall. Likewise, God reaches out and accompanies his children on every step they take through life. Christians love and trust God, for he won't let them fall and miss out on the blessings and happiness offered.

... GOD'S PLAN IS...

HAPPINESS!

INVESTIGATION
NOTES

◆ ◆ ◆

MORE USEFUL WORDS

Apostles: the twelve followers of Jesus, who were chosen to be his closest disciples.

Baptism: a Christian rite of sprinkling or being immersed in water, symbolizing entering the Church.

Blessings: wishing happiness for others.

Communion: a close relationship with God and other Christians; the act of taking bread and wine.

Creation: the beginning of the universe and all living things, including human life. Christians believe God is the creator.

Day of Judgment: an act of examining thoughts and deeds by God at the end of times.

Evangelist: a writer of a Gospel. The word comes from the Greek meaning "the good news", and the focus is on telling the life and teachings of Jesus.

Faith: a spiritual confidence and trust in a set of beliefs of a religion, rather than proof.

Fall: a disastrous separation between God and humans, each other, and the environment caused by sin. God plans a rescue.

Forgiveness or absolution: a complete release from guilt or punishment.

Incarnation: Jesus is God in human flesh: true God and true man.

Kingdom of God: a vision of life lived in the way that God intends for all people; Jesus sets an example, inspiring others to follow with the help of God's Spirit.

Liturgical: relating to words and practices for public worship.

Prophecy: a message from God received by a prophet.

Resurrection: the raising from death to life.

Sacrifice: an offering to an unseen higher power that often involves killing an animal or a person.

Wisdom: wise words based on knowledge, experience, and understanding.

Worship: an act of showing adoration and praise to God.

Index

The references given relate to the chapter numbers.

Illustration Credits

Illustrations of Sophie and Thomas: Sophie Chaussade

Other illustrations: Marie Bretin

Illustrations shutterstock.com : page 55 © sdp_creations, page 67 © Morphart Creation